THE POWER OF CREDIT

PRESENTS

LIVING THE

DREAM

TONY SANTOS

THE POWER OF CREDIT PUBLISHING

POWEROFCREDIT.COM

THE POWER OF CREDIT PRESENTS...LIVING THE DREAM.

A COMPREHENSIVE GUIDE FOR THE CREATIVES AND DREAMERS OF THE WORLD ON HOW TO USE THE POWER OF CREDIT TO HELP MAKE THEIR DREAMS COME TRUE.

BROUGHT TO YOU BY THE SAME AUTHOR THAT WROTE THE BOOK: THE POWER OF CREDIT IS IN YOUR HANDS.

THE POWER OF CREDIT PUBLISHING

POWER OF CREDIT PUBLISHING

CHICAGO, ILLINOIS

2020

TABLE OF CONTENTS

Power of Credit LLC

Mission Statement

Our Mission here at Power of Credit is to empower the communities to understand the importance of credit worthiness, wealth building and financial independence through education, access, planning and execution.

We are set out to help the people of the community to enhance their, quality of life by improving their credit rating, building assets, establishing financial stability and developing generational wealth to be passed on from generation to generation.

DEDICATION

First and foremost, I would like to dedicate this book to my Heavenly Father God. He has blessed me in more ways than I can count. He has saved my life more times than I can remember. He has blessed me with the ability to create and turn my dreams into reality. Thank You God.

I without a doubt would love to thank my beautiful wife Mrs. Tambria Knighten Santos. She has stood by my side through thick and thin. She has inspired me to be a better man and grow into the God-loving and fearing man I am today. Love you, Doll Face.

It is a must that I dedicate this book to my kids. All that I do is for them. They saved my life when I was lost, and they motivate me to be great now that I am found. Love you all. Antonia, Tyler, Taylor, Antowine, Michael and Amelia.

I also would like to dedicate this to my loving and caring mother Jenny Santos. She raised me with unconditional love. She never turned her back on me even through my darkest days. Love you Mom.

I cannot forget my Pops, David Torres. He took me in and raised me as his own. He instilled the toughness in me that is needed to survive in this very cruel world. Thanks Pops; love you.

To my brothers and sisters whom I love dearly. They gave me the respect of a big brother and allowed me to learn what it means to be a true leader. Love you all.

To my brother Larry Jones who has helped me more times than I can remember. Every time I came up with some wild idea, he was right there to help me pursue it. He never switched up on me and remained loyal. Love you my brother. (Everybody is not little Larry).

To my big brother John Carter, thank you for showing me what being a real man is about. A perfect example to follow, a true inspiration, and the most genuine person I know. You took me in when my world fell apart and helped me to get back on my feet and helped me be the man I am today. Love you big bro.

Steve Butler, the Big Boss. You gave me a chance when most people did not. You helped me pursue my goals and dreams. You helped me to believe in myself and see that higher levels of success are real and inspired me to reach them. Love you, Boss man.

Mr. Levar Berry. The man behind the curtains that makes great things happen. One of the smartest people I know and a huge part of me chasing the levels most people do not know exist. You helped me to shift my mindset, focus, and direction. I have leveled up because of you. Thank you for believing in me and my mission. Love you Sir.

To Dennis Round. You know who you are. I am honored to call you a friend. You have reignited a fire in me that began to die out. You gave me hope that the level I am chasing is obtainable and that the locked doors can be open. Love you bro.

Lesley Martinez, you are greatly appreciated for all you have done for me. You helped me to become a published author and make one of my dreams come true. Thank you for your continuous guidance and support. Love you ma'am.

Seandale Hunley (Brother Dale). You are a great man who has helped me in many ways. I appreciate your love, support and brotherhood throughout the years. You have shown me that the next level is real and can be reached. Love you Brother.

Special thanks to my Santos Family, my Torres Family, the Martinez Family, Christian Rodriguez, Philip Oliveras, Jay Dones, Tony Russell, John Bluford, Donnell Cummings, Perry Perelman, Guy Petropolous, Mr. Starks and to my friends and family who have supported my 1000's of dreams and ideas. Who have believed in me even during times when I did not believe in myself. To all the wonderful people who I have crossed paths with. Thank you all and GOD BLESS!!!!!

To you the reader. Thank you for your time and attention. I am honored to be able to enter your world and grateful for the opportunity to share my knowledge and thoughts with you. My all your dreams come true.

God Bless You All!!!!!

INTRODUCTION

I WISH I WOULD HAVE KNOWN.

Growing up, I always considered myself a dreamer, my head full of ideas and goals and future accomplishments. Inspired by the movie Backdraft, I someday saw myself as a firefighter or a first responder, a real hero ready to save lives. With that inspiration in my heart, I joined the military at the age of seventeen and trained to become a combat medic. As life so often happens, however, that career did not pan out. Eighteen was a great age to be a medic in Texas, not so much in Illinois where the age requirement was twenty-one. Derailed, my life drifted in another direction. A short while later, I became blinded by the bright lights of Hollywood as I was introduced to the arts: music and theater. Presented with the opportunities by Mr. Johnny Brown to act in several stage-plays and record some of my own original music, the big lights of Hollywood seemed within reach. One of my fondest memories is that of performing in front of a crowd of about one hundred people, basking in their applause as I received a standing ovation for my hard work and effort. Surely I thought a star was born that night, and that belief was solidified when people asked me for my autograph. My autograph! Never had I signed one, never thought I would, but the feeling was astonishing. The effects of such a night lingered, as I never completely lost the desire to perform and create art. Again, as life so often goes, that dream got put on hold as I grew up, got older, and my responsibilities grew right along with me. A few years passed before I pursued that particular dream again. At this point in time, I was the proud owner of my own business The Equator: a clothing store that transformed from a few items being sold out of the back of my car trunk to a thriving brick-and-mortar operation. Opening that business allowed me to pursue life as an artist once more, although not as a "starving-artist", thankfully. A small, two-bedroom apartment at the back of my one-thousand square foot store was where I lived. It was in this apartment that my desire to become a rap-artist was reignited. Turning the pantry into a studio booth and my living room into an engineering room, I was able to record quite the music catalog that unfortunately never saw the light of day. I did eventually give up on the dream of being an actor or rap-artist, but not before I met some interesting people, experienced some growing pains, and learned a lot of valuable lessons. I have come to appreciate such growths as parts of the beauty of life, however, I have come to the realization that "chasing the dream" was not and is not as easy as it seems.

One of the biggest lessons I learned was how to fund those dreams through the POWER OF CREDIT. I will share more on how I figured that out as we go through this book. I cannot count how many times I wish I did not give up and would have instead continued pursuing my dreams, especially those of being an actor – I was really good at it if I say so myself. (For real I was lol). Furthermore, I cannot tell you how many times I have said "I WISH I WOULD'VE KNOWN." How differently would any of our lives be if we knew then, what we know now?

With that being said, the purpose of this book is to help the next aspiring artist or creative be able to chase their dream as relentlessly as I wanted to chase mine. I will be sharing valuable information, hard lessons I have learned, and powerful knowledge with you in the hopes that it will not only help you chase your dreams, but help you fulfill those dreams as well. Life is filled with ups and downs, goals, dreams, and aspirations and the fact that you are reading this book is PROOF that DREAMS DO COME TRUE. Mines did and yours can too.

Download The Power of Credit App to enhance your reading of this book.

CHAPTER 1
CHASING THE DREAM

CHASING THE DREAM

Life is about more than the norm; it is bigger and better than the average, and this is how I have always felt. Perhaps my thinking is also different than the norm and less aligned with the thoughts of others. For me, however, life is about more than the 9-5 cycle: wake up, go to work, come home, eat, sleep, and repeat. Every day the cycle repeats, until the age of 65 if one is lucky enough to retire at that age. Look how many of our elders are still required to work in order to survive. That cycle is not one that sits well with me, and how can it? This cycle demands that we trade our time – *priceless, valuable, never-to-return-again time* – for money. At the end of the day, it is not a fair trade if you ask me. Time cannot be regained when given away, as once it is gone, it is gone forever. *Energy, like time, is also too valuable to give away.* Allowing someone to put a price tag on my invaluable time, energy, effort, knowledge, and work ethic is just not something I can easily stand. If I were to allow someone to monetize such precious resources, it would not be for minimum wage and it would not be for a long period of time.

Throughout my youth, I had numerous opportunities to earn money in atypical fashions. I did not work a typical 9-5, where I would only be compensated for my efforts every two weeks. Instead, exposure to entrepreneurship allowed me to obtain money daily, rather than biweekly, giving me a taste of freedom from the corporate timeline. There was no "paycheck-to-paycheck" living because money was available at any moment, I decided to work for it. It was during these stints of making money through my own ideas that I learned what money is. Not only what it is, but how to best obtain it for myself, without the parameters set by others. I was my own Boss and made my own decisions. I could make more money through my own ideas and merits than I ever could with a salaried job. These beliefs were solidified by my upbringing, growing up as the "different kid" who did not quite fit in. I was abrasive, defiant, stubborn, and never cool enough for the "in crowd". Stubbornness led to the questioning of authorities and norms that did not make sense to me. Like any young person, it took some time, but I accepted my differences and learned to embrace them. Growing up in an urban environment, where poverty, crime, and violence ran rampant, perspectives on what values are important in life are often skewed. How could they not? A home with no father, a security net of government assistance, and watching your mother struggle can alter perceptions and help dictate decisions. To escape that, what would you do? For many of my peers, the answer sought out included lifestyles that did not mesh with what I really wanted. My environment, coupled with my own inner quirks, allowed me to determine that I needed better than what I had. Not only did I need better, I needed to become better. A thirst for greatness was awakened in my youth and I had to achieve it through following my dreams, whatever they may be. Throughout my life, I have had the incomparable pleasure of knowing what it feels like to achieve a dream. Unfortunately, I can speak on the indescribable pain that accompanies having dreams crushed. Both experiences being priceless and irreplaceable. The journey down the road to success is filled with so many challenges, roadblocks, and obstacles, it is normal to second guess yourself. Perhaps even take a third, fourth, and fifth guess as well. Whatever the journey may be, I can attest that mine was not smooth sailing, not at all what it was cracked up to be, and not for the faint of heart. Commitment to pursuing your goals will test your limits, push you to the edge of sanity, lure you back with promises of victory, and repeat. Personally, my trails could fill a book on its own, crafting a story that would make you cringe or cry, if not both. As a diamond is created under pressure, my life has pressured me into becoming someone stronger, as evidenced by my words written here. If I had allowed that pressure to crumble me instead, I would not be here now, sharing my thoughts, experiences, struggles, and truths with you. ***PERSEVERANCE and DETERMINATION*** have become my greatest allies, allowing me to wake up every day when my world feels like it has ended or about to end, and urging me to always do the next right thing.

The life of an entrepreneur has been set in stone for me. No matter what new obstacles pop up, what setbacks I experience, or doubts that creep, there is no turning back for me. I have spent decades pursuing this lifestyle, and I will either make my dreams happen, or die trying, as failure cannot be an option and is not one. For me, chasing the dream is what life is about; the journey, the path chosen, and the things experienced on the way are the fillings of life, with the success at the end like a cherry on top. Setting goals – especially those deemed impossible by others – can make the taste of victory that much sweeter.

It cannot be done.

You are wasting your time.

Why would you do that?

(I feed off those words like fire does wood).

Learning to turn these doubts into affirmations is a crucial step in realizing that you truly can be whatever you wish to be. ***Impossibilities are simply possibilities that have not been achieved yet.*** As I have urged myself to do every day, I now implore you to do whatever it takes to reach your goals. It will take sacrifice and time, but the outcomes will be worth it. Take your time, but do not waste it, as time is precious. Deny negativity and do not let others and their fears alter your course. ***With only this life to live, chase your dreams with all your might.***

CHASING THE DREAM!

CHAPTER 2
BALANCE IS THE KEY

BALANCE IS KEY

This chapter is going to be an interesting delve into my mental growth over the years. To begin, I spent a good portion of my life living as a Hustler, then an Entrepreneur and now a Businessman. The pace was fast, dizzying, with a "pedal-to-the-metal" mindset that told me I had to make it big and do it now. My twenties and thirties were consumed by this framework of thought, and in retrospect, although I would not want to change this mentality, bits of wisdom tell me that I should. Why? To put it frank, I was judgmental towards people who thought differently than I. Judgment would couple with condescension, leading me to look down on others who simply wanted salaried careers and the norm. If you didn't want more for yourself, I didn't like you.

The frustration of not understanding their thinking would drive me crazy, to the point that I would discredit those who wanted to pursue higher education. I was once given the opportunity to speak at a seminar at my son's school regarding financial literacy. I was a member of a panel that included a teacher, the principal, and a mental health physician. When my turn to present came around, I started my speech with "School is for dummies." Remember when I said I was abrasive in my youth? Well, I guess some of that quality followed me into adulthood. As you can imagine, I ruffled quite a lot of feathers in the crowd with that statement. However, I felt justified! How could taking out thousands of dollars in student loans, simply to get a job to pay back those loans, be the smarter, more lucrative decision? Seeing so many people take out loans for a degree that they then could not even utilize drove me to the conclusion that college cannot be the right choice. It did not help that data seemed to agree with me. The student debt crisis is frequently in the news, and individuals with master's degrees are retail workers and baristas. While there is nothing wrong with working in customer service, I think everyone can agree that it is not worth thousands of dollars in loans.

Fortunately, time has opened my eyes to my own prejudices and judgmental ideas, allowing me to alter my thinking for the better. I can now appreciate the merits of pursuing higher education, as that degree truly can open doors. During one of the many bumps along my journey to financial independence, circumstances dictated that I work a number of odd jobs in order to make ends meet. These odd jobs strengthened my belief that the 9-5 lifestyle was not for me, but they also made me realize that I would never benefit from the perks that came with these jobs. There would be no health insurance, guaranteed income, IRA contributions and 401k's. So, things began to click; there was a sense of security that those around me sought through these jobs and careers. Since that form of security would never be mine, I had to make my own, which meant doing whatever it would take to ensure my financial future.

The shift of my mindset can be attributed to valuable lessons learned from those closest to me. My wife is one of those who had helped me to change my judgmental thinking and she has done it in such a simple way. Every time I would get on my high horse, my wife has helped to bring me back down to earth, often telling me that everybody does not have to think the way I do. Further, their different beliefs and ideas does not mean they are wrong. Her constant patience and her determination to keep me grounded and humble forced me to do some introspection. Reflecting on my past behavior and thoughts has revealed that I went about things the wrong way. There is no clear-cut roadmap to success or a blueprint to wealth. Therefore, just as I often had to struggle and learn lessons the hard way, those who I have misjudged are also carving their own roads as well. This lesson was further strengthened by witnessing the success of my own younger brother. As a blue-collar worker, my brother David Torres is the 9-5 "average Joe" I would so erroneously look down on. His work ethic is unquestioningly admirable, however, and when he came to me for assistance in improving his credit, I knew I had to help. My brother was able to use the framework for credit repair I created after years of study and trial-and-error, and with that framework, he became a first-time homeowner with little money down and stellar financing. Watching him grind day-in and day-out to achieve his goals allowed me to see that there are multiple paths to success. Proud of you bro.

My family has not only shown me that there are multiple paths to achieving goals, but that the journey is not a race. I have twin sons who allowed me to guide them laying the groundwork for their financial success. When they turned eighteen, I advised them to immediately begin building their credit history by opening a *secured credit card.* This is such a great way to build credit history and it proved successful for my sons. Before their twentieth birthdays, both of my sons had credit lines worth over ten-thousand dollars. One son was able to use his now-stellar credit to purchase his first car. His accomplishment felt as if it were my own. The ability to help your children do better than yourself is amazing. I was unable to finance a new car until later in life and my son beat me by a decade or so, ***breaking a generational curse.*** The lessons learned from my family can be summed up as this: it is vital to have balance in your life. The late Nipsey Hustle, a musician, celebrity entrepreneur and community leader, said it best: ***"Life is a marathon."*** Instead of running yourself ragged and burning out, it is best to pace yourself. Do not be afraid to create a game plan that may span months or years; pursue your goals at your own pace. The important thing is that your goals are accomplished, not necessarily when. Now, that does not mean you should waste time, but also be sure to take care of yourself to prevent burnout. ***Take care of your mental, physical, emotional, spiritual, and financial health.*** Ensuring your all-around health will aid you in fulfilling whatever destiny awaits you. Of course, this is not easy to do when income is insecure, and you do not know where your next dollar or meal is going to come from. Such insecurity can be stressful and take a toll on you mentally. Trust me I know. With that in mind, I frequently tell my clients that there is nothing wrong with getting a job; and I am going to share that same sentiment with you, my readers. Having a steady source of income can relieve a lot of pressure and stress while chasing your goals. Stay focused but allow yourself some stability.

Knowing what I know now, if I could go back in time I would certainly get a job, work at it for a few years to aid me in building my credit, and then use that credit to buy a property. That property would in turn be used to build more wealth. The way I see it, punching a clock is no longer a terrible idea, especially when you have an exit strategy in place. *If you are going to work, make sure you hustle for a cause and not just because.* Use your job to create opportunities for growth because it is crucial to find balance between what you want to do and what you must do. To wrap this chapter up, I know now that pursuing higher education is a smart move as well. My past self was rash when it came to misjudging a college education. I urge you to consider taking classes that are related to your interests and your goals. Perfect your craft. Education also consists of studying others who have done what you are trying to do and learning from them. Even if you do not enroll in school, pick up a book on what you want to do and read it. **Knowledge is Power**, and the more you know, the more you can grow. Be balanced enough in your choices and endeavors so that you can withstand the tough times and are knowledgeable enough to have safety nets in place. **Take a calculated risk** and go for it all because balance is key.

CHAPTER 3
GUARANTEE YOUR SUCCESS

GUARANTEE
YOUR SUCCESS

I hate to be the bearer of bad news, but nobody is going to believe in you if you do not believe in yourself. It is imperative that you know that your goals are achievable and that you can and will be what you want to be. **Confidence can be seen a mile away**; it is magnetic and contagious, attracting the attention of those around you. When you know what you are doing and are knowledgeable on what you are discussing, others will be drawn to you and will want to listen. This makes it important to surround yourself with the right people. If you are the smartest, most accomplished person at your table, then you are sitting at the wrong table. Being the smartest person in the room entails never learning more and it is time to leave that room. Do not cap yourself; be confident enough to step into bigger rooms and sit at grander tables. A wise woman once told me to never walk into a room on your knees. To always walk with your head high chest out and **REMEMBER WHO YOU ARE!!!!!**

I spent countless years of my life urging others to see my vision and to share my dreams, essentially begging them to share my ideals. I learned the hard way that the urging and begging was pointless and impossible. **It must be understood that your dreams are your dreams.** Your goals, aspirations, and ideas belong solely to you. Given that, it is an unavoidable fact that not everybody is going to believe in you and your dreams. Another hard lesson to learn is that it is completely fine for people to hold that opinion; they do not have to believe in you. The only person who must have one-hundred percent faith in your aspirations, is **YOU**. I learned these lessons and accepted them, and I hope you do too. Realizing that you do not need the affirmation of others can be freeing; this realization helped me to realize that it was up to me to get things done. This led to me becoming *MY OWN INVESTOR!!!!!*

Well, how do you become your own investor? I am sure that is your next question and I'm here to answer that question. It took a lot of time to figure out this formula. To say that it happened overnight would be a lie, as it took years of let downs and disappointments to figure out how to invest in myself. False hopes, broken promises, lies and betrayals, they sound like something out of a soap opera or telenovela lol. Unfortunately, the people who may come into your life to take advantage of you are far from fantasy. These were even harder lessons I am grateful to have learned, however, because they only served to strengthen my resolve in myself and in those who matter.

The difficult part of trying to do the impossible is that there can be an overwhelming lack of proper resources and support. The primary resource, of course, being money. Lack of money is at the heart of the problem, limiting what you can do and setting the boundaries on what is possible and what is impossible. Money is a necessity that is needed in order, for you to invest in yourself, your business, your welfare, and everything else in life. Hard to start a business when you are hungry, right? You get the picture; money is one of the main resources you will need to make almost any dream come true.

Now, this is where the real fun begins. You know you need the money, so here is how to get it and become **YOUR OWN INVESTOR.** Ready? Because here comes the magic potion, the special word to unlock and open the door of opportunity, and the best kept secret: **CREDIT.** Let me say it again for you **CREDIT.** To be specific, your **PERSONAL CREDIT**, because that asset is going to be your best one. Both **PERSONAL CREDIT AND BUSINESS CREDIT** can be used to turn your dreams into reality.

The first step on your quest for success is making sure that your personal credit is where **LENDERS** want it to be. Your initial focus should be on strengthening your **PERSONAL CREDIT FILE** as much as possible. This does not mean simply raising your FICO score; no, we want the credit file itself – the loan and payment histories, inquiries, collections, income-to-debt ratios, etc. to be picture perfect, or as close as possible.

INVESTING IN YOUR PERSONAL CREDIT will be one of the smartest moves you can ever make. Although this seems easier said than done, it can be a difficult process that is beyond worth taking. It is necessary. Fortunately, for those who may not have stellar credit histories, there is no such thing as **CREDIT THAT CANNOT BE FIXED**. So regardless of what your credit file looks like now, you can take the steps to get it where it needs to be.

If you do not know why I am telling you this, it is simple. Banks and lenders do not want to loan large amounts of money to a person with **BAD OR WEAK CREDIT**. They want to get their money back, and your credit history is an indicator of how likely they are going to have their funds returned to them. Another thing to note is that most banks and lenders will not give large sums to new businesses (if that worries you, fear not, we will touch more on that in the next chapter). Therefore, having good or great credit will grant you access to the capital that you need to purchase equipment and materials, travel, market your business or brand, pay bills, and meet other expenses that may arise. *Leverage your credit to help facilitate your process.*

With all that, being said, let us go over the first steps in getting your personal credit on track and ready for life's marathon. *The absolute first step in all of this is knowing where your credit is at.* We cannot improve it if we do not know what it looks like to begin with, right? Fortunately, there are, a number of tools you can use to take a peek at your file. Many people are familiar with Credit Karma, and I personally believe it is a fine website to use. Be warned, however, that there are three agencies – or bureaus – that keep track of your credit, and Credit Karma only allows access to two out of the three of those credit bureaus reports. You need access to all three reports from **TransUnion, Equifax, and Experian**. Through Credit Karma, you will only receive TransUnion and Equifax reports. This is important to consider because the information being reported to each of these bureaus differs; what is reported to Equifax may not be reported to TransUnion and so-on. Furthermore, Credit Karma utilizes a scoring system known as Vantage, whereas **most lenders use the FICO scoring system**.

To make matters more complicated, the two scoring systems will generate two different scores for your file. In a nutshell, we perhaps need to find another source to view all three reports.

Step one:

OBTAIN A THREE BUREAUS CREDIT REPORT.

You can do this by downloading the Power of Credit mobile app if you do not already have it. In the app, I have provided a link to a recommended credit monitoring site.

Click on *FREE CREDIT ANALYSIS, within the app will reveal this link. Then, clicking on the link will take you to a page where you will be invited to set up an account, granting you access to your three bureaus credit report.

*Please note, it is also possible to request your free report, as everyone is entitled to one free report per year from each of the three companies. Go to freeannualcreditreport.com to get a copy of your report from each bureau.

Step two:

GET A FREE DETAILED CREDIT ANALYSIS.

To do this, go back to the Power of Credit mobile app and click on FREE ANALYSIS. Fill out the required fields and someone from my team will email you a complementary Detailed Credit Analysis. This analysis will break down and highlight all of the negative and inaccurate information that is being reported by creditors and lenders to the credit bureaus. This analysis will be detailed, easy to understand, and filled with powerful information. I recommend that you read it several times, study it, learn from it, and attempt to understand every component.

Step Three:

After receiving and reviewing your Detailed Credit Analysis, I recommend setting up an appointment for **A PERSONALIZED CREDIT CONSULTATION.** If this prospect interests you, go back to the Power of Credit mobile app and click on **SCHEDULE CONSULTATION.** Pick a time and day that is available and someone from my team will comb through your credit file with you.

This grants you a free, thirty minute personalized and detailed review of your credit file. Expect the consultant to explain what it is you can do to get your credit on track and in order, for you to qualify for funding. Together, we will formulate a plan of action designed specifically around your current credit status and goals.

Step Four:

Now that you have received your credit analysis, consultation, and personalized plan of action, it is time to decide, commit, and execute said plan.

If you have negative marks on your reports – such as collections, late payments, charge-offs, bankruptcies, repossessions, foreclosures, etc. – we must work on getting those items removed from your credit report.

In the back of this book, under the resources section, I have provided one of the best letters you can use to accomplish this. If you are not comfortable addressing these negative or inaccurate items on your own, do not hesitate to reach out. *My team and I at* **Power of Credit, LLC** *are here to help you.* **Beyond the negative marks, if you are using more than 30% of your available credit, that too can harm your credit score and file.**

Formulate a plan and put it into action to pay down those balances; no matter how small you start. **Baby steps are better than no steps.** Doing this will give your credit score a significant boost because **CREDIT UTILIZATION** – how much you use your credit cards and how high your balances are – accounts for **30% of your credit score**. Be proactive, follow the plan of action tailored for you, and you will see tremendous results.

I cannot emphasize enough the importance of getting your personal credit in order. Make the investment into your credit and know that it is worth every dollar. Furthermore, I implore you to change your mindset, on credit through educating yourself on how vital it is for your financial health. If you understand how it works and why it is so important, it can save you a great amount of money in the future (I could write another book on interest rates and the pitfalls surrounding them). Fix your personal credit and you can *"SECURE THE BAG"*

Your credit must be financeable in order, to secure the funding needed to help you accomplish your goals. Most banks and lenders are not going to give you any money if you cannot personally guarantee that you will pay it back. ***A PERSONAL GUARANTOR***, also known as a ***PG,*** is mandatory in order, to obtain financing for almost every lender. This is, why I have titled this chapter

"Guarantee Your Success" because it is up to you to make the conscious decision to get your credit in order. Do this, and I assure you that you will be one major step closer to achieving your goals.

I have had the privilege to help many people accomplish their goals with the process we previously discussed. I have seen people go from nothing to **LIVING THE DREAM** within a short period of time. From renters to homeowners, from 9-5 workers to business owners, from artists making music in their bedrooms and basements to making music in their brand new music studios. I have witnessed it all. Being able to take part in the process of helping someone make their dreams come true is a dream come true for myself. Therefore, trust and believe that this process works, and I hope to someday share in your joy and success as well.

TRUST THE PROCESS.

TRUST THE SYSTEM.

TRUST YOURSELF.

I designed the Power of Credit Mobile App to be a tool that can be used on the journey to accomplish your goals and well beyond.

I strongly recommend reading my first book The Power of Credit is in Your Hands. It is a great book that is filled with valuable information and secrets of the credit industry. It will help you to better understand your credit and how to use it properly to fund your goals and dreams.

GUARANTEE YOUR SUCCESS!

CHAPTER 4

UNLOCK THE DOORS

UNLOCK THE DOORS

As discussed in the previous chapter, making your dreams come true is solely your responsibility. It is all on you. We know that sitting around waiting for someone else to make our dreams come true is not conducive. If we did that, we would be waiting an eternity. I will reiterate again, remember that you can make your dreams come true. Believe in your capabilities. That is the entire purpose of this book, to help you make your dreams become reality.

It took me a long time to transition from hustler to businessman, and to be honest, I am still learning the ins and outs of that role. I attribute parts of my success on my ability to visualize and create. If I can see something with my mind's eye, I can bring it to life, and that ability has been a blessing, allowing me to accomplish some of my biggest goals. *I also pay special attention to my dreams because they are the mind's way of helping you to problem solve and attain.* I dreamed about writing my first book, developing my mobile app, becoming a real estate investor, and opening my office. I even had a dream about writing this book! I believe that *God speaks to us in our dreams*, but even if you are not religious, your brain has amazing abilities to help consolidate information and problem solve while dreaming! Dreams have meanings, you simply must be aware enough to pay attention.

Because some of my best ideas come to me in the, midst of my dreams, I make sure to keep a pen and paper on my nightstand. When a particularly inspiring dream hits me, I will jot down as much as I can remember so I can recall it the next morning. Believe it or not, this method has worked for me many times. *I transform my visions and dreams into words on paper, and once they are out of my head, I can manifest those dreams in the real world. I turn dreams into words, words (ideas) into goals, goals into plans, plans into actions, and actions into fruitions.* Such a simple step has allowed me to create my own windows of opportunity and unlock doors that were previously closed.

The theme of this chapter is all about doors; I opened the door by creating my own. What does that look like? For one thing, I started **MY OWN LLC and OPENED MY OWN BUSINESS**. In the grand scheme of things, the upfront cost was minimal, although it varies from state to state. No matter what industry or field your goals may be in, you should begin by turning it into a business. The feeling of opening your own business and seeing the name of your business on official documents – called *Articles of Incorporation* – can light a fire within you that will lead to another level of motivation. That motivation can be turned into focus that will drive you further.

The nice thing about starting a business is that it is not as difficult as you might think. Regardless, whatever the cost, it will be an investment worth making. *The day that you start your own LLC will mark the official start of your dreams becoming reality.* Furthermore, there are quite a few benefits in opening an LLC. First and foremost, your business will be its **OWN SEPARATE ENTITY** meaning you can now establish what is known as **BUSINESS CREDIT or CORPORATE CREDIT**, benefit from tax credits, and most importantly obtain *FUNDING and FINANCING.* The amounts that you can finance through your business are typically larger than those that can be attained using your personal credit. These are just the tip of the iceberg regarding the benefits of having an LLC.

When opening your business, you want to be sure that it is *STRUCTURED CORRECTLY*. When obtaining financing, the structure of your business will be evaluated and plays an important role in getting approved. Therefore, *a correctly structured business increases your odds of approval.* Lenders want to rest assured that they are dealing with a legitimate, professional company, not something that was haphazardly thrown together. They seek confidence in you and your business's ability to pay them back. Below, I have provided a *BUSINESS CREDIT CHECKLIST* that will help you to properly structure your business. Follow this checklist and make sure you have each step completed before trying to get financing.

BUSINESS CREDIT CHECKLIST

1. *Formulate a name, address, and start date of the business.*
2. *Register the business with the Secretary of State.*
3. *Obtain an EIN/tax ID from the IRS*
4. *Create a phone line for business use only*
5. *Register the phone number with 411*
6. *Create a professional business email*

7. *Develop a website*
8. *Open a business bank account*
9. *Get a merchant account to accept credit/debit card payments*

*Note: The following are also highly recommended.

Create a professional voicemail

Obtain a fax and 1-800 number

Design a logo

Obtain a professional license (If Required).

The reason I titled the last chapter **"Guarantee Your Success"** *is because, even for business credit financing, you have, to personally guarantee that the business is going to pay back any loans taken out.* Now, there are ways to establish your business credit without having to be a personal guarantor. What most people are unaware of is that you can establish business credit using only the **EIN** of the business and **NOT** your **Social Security Number.** There is a step-by-step process that you must go through and it is not one that can be completed overnight. In all actuality, this process can take up to 6 to 12 months to truly start establishing your business credit. I will provide a few of those steps in the resources section of the book. It will guide you through the beginning steps that will allow you to start building business credit as soon as the first day of starting your LLC.

The overall goal is to have both your Personal and Business Credit where you need them to be because both will be able to stand on their own and secure the financing you will need. Combining both your Personal and Business Credit are like suddenly gaining superpowers. It is also possible to work on building both at the same time. I have had plenty of clients establish both their Personal and Business Credit simultaneously. Doing this saves valuable time.

By creating your own business, you are creating and unlocking your own doors of opportunity. Doing this will put you on the map and put you in the game. For years, I felt as if I were Kobe, sitting on the bench, begging to be put in the game. I knew I was good, and I was ready. Life never put me in the game, so I created my own team. If you are in the game, you have a chance to win; sitting on the couch watching the game will never lead to victory. Steve Harvey once said, *"If you do not jump, you will not fall, but if you do not jump, you will not fly either."*

Because it does not take as much money as you may think to make this happen, investing in your personal credit is the crucial first step. Get your personal credit straight and you can get financing. Obtain financing and now you can use those funds to invest in your business and business credit. Following the plan, once your business credit is established, you can obtain even more financing and use those funds to further invest in your business. That financing can help you purchase your supplies and equipment, pay for orders, invest in marketing, and truly grow your business. *Whatever it is that you want to do, you can use your credit – both Personal and Business – to be your own investor and invest in yourself.*

You can start receiving financing in as little as 30 to 90 days from when you start. There are ways to boost your personal credit that will expedite the process. Look up Credit Piggybacking and do some research on adding authorized user tradelines. It is an industry secret on how to raise your credit score significantly and quickly.

THE KEYS ARE NOW IN YOUR HANDS THAT YOU NEED TO.

UNLOCK THE DOORS!

CHAPTER 5
INVEST IN YOURSELF

INVEST IN YOURSELF

Investing your time and energy into building both your personal and business credit will be one of the best investments you could possibly make. Your credit will be your biggest asset and your best investor, unlocking doors that otherwise would forever be shut. Once you establish your personal credit, many funding programs are available through **CREDIT CARD COMPANIES and CREDIT UNIONS** that will assist in the next step of building business credit. Past clients of mine have been able to secure **HUNDREDS OF THOUSANDS OF DOLLARS IN UNSECURED FINANCING** through such programs, allowing their personal credit to leverage funds to start a business and develop business credit. Think about that, within six months to a year, clients were able to receive financing without offering up collateral, allowing them to achieve business credit funding. What can be done with that business credit? Well, I have seen barber-shops open, clothing stores built, music studios established, houses purchased, trucking fleets started, and dreams become reality. The initial investments into their personal credit paved the way for these clients to accomplish the goals they set in place.

Leveraging your credit is the way to put yourself in business and become your own boss, giving you options and opportunities that may have not been available beforehand. **Now do not get me wrong, it is a big risk. Using your credit does not mean "free money" as the loans and debts must be paid back**. The minute you take out a loan or swipe a credit card, a bill is generated that you are responsible for paying. If the loans are not paid back and, more importantly, **PAID ON TIME,** all the work you just put into your credit will be wasted. One missed payment can and will kill your credit rating so having a game plan in place is critical to the success of your business. ***Ensure the health of your credit by having a repayment plan in place and following through with it.***

As with all business endeavors, there are risks and rewards; therefore, it is crucial to ask yourself: what are the risks of this choice? What are the potential rewards? Which will outweigh the other? These are questions I ask myself frequently and my answers to these questions help determine my next steps. It is simple, if the risks outweigh the rewards, why bother? If the potential rewards outweigh the risks, then go for it. This does not mean to be afraid to take risks, however, especially when it comes to making your first move. ***When you start at the bottom, what do you truly have to lose?*** If something does not pan out, you may return to square one, but you were there to begin with. Again, this does not mean I condone jumping out of a plane without a parachute. The idea behind the madness is that you truly must take **CALCULATED RISK**. I put emphasis on the word calculated because it is critical that you do your research. Learn the ins-and-outs of what it is you wish to accomplish and do the math. If things add up, do not hesitate to pull the trigger. ***This means that you must plan accordingly, because if you fail to plan then you are planning to fail.***

Now what happens if you do fail? Taking, a look at others can help us answer that question. Some of the best sports teams in history have lost games yet gone on to win championships; some of the most successful individuals have experienced failure. The nice thing about defeat is that the heart of it sets you up for some of life's best lessons. Michael Jordan was cut from his basketball team; Kobe Bryant shot airballs during a critical playoff game; Tom Brady blew a perfect season and lost during the Super Bowl. What do they all have in common, beyond their failures, is that they all bounced back better than ever, Furthermore, *the only true failures in life are those that result without any lessons being learned.*

The reward of opening your own business, becoming your own boss, controlling your own destiny, and creating your own legacy is, in my opinion, a risk that **MUST** be taken. Breaking ***GENERATIONAL CURSES, building GENERATIONAL WEALTH***, and living the life you want to live is worth the risk. The harsh reality is that the majority, of us are not born with silver spoons in our mouths, let alone a gold one; we were not born rich. So, we must grind, we must take some chances, take some losses, and continuously fall on our backs. But we must do these things in order, to learn how to get back up. Recognize that returning to square one is not the end of the world. We all must figure life out the best way we know how, and I hope that sharing with you what I have learned thus far will be beneficial. Fortunately, I have seen the things I know work for myself, my friends, and my family, the same way that it has worked for millions of others. Far from being the inventor of these methods, I am merely one who was blessed enough to discover them.

I have heard that if one is born poor, it is not their fault, but if they die poor, they have none to blame but themselves. This has led me to take whatever steps are necessary to pursue my goals and now I task you with the same. Invest in your credit and take control of your goals. Make, a plan, do your research, and do not fear taking risks. Remember, nobody will believe in you the way that you can believe in yourself, so believe that your goals will happen, make them happen, and make others believe it too. A good friend once told me *"Do the possible and watch God help you do the impossible."*

INVEST IN YOURSELF!

CHAPTER 6
BUILD YOUR CASTLE

2'11"

49'9"

67'3"

BUILD THE CASTLE

For years I lived in a *"Cash is King"* world, where every move I made was about making money. I would grind from sunup until sundown, day in and day out. There was no 24/7 for me and I would frequently tell people that I worked 25/8. This all stemmed from the determination to make as much money as possible, and oftentimes, I did. I honestly made a lot of money in my lifetime. I was blessed enough to earn up to twenty-thousand dollars a week from my clothing business alone. That determination to make money further stemmed from the strong desire to never live as poorly as I did as a youth. I did not want to ever be in a position where government assistance was all I had to rely on. Dying poor was not an option either. I know I am not the only person out there who has the same drives and the same mindset, but it was not until one of my dreams came crashing down that I realized that mentality was not the best. I would often say "I can sleep when I die". The work until you drop mentality is wrong. I was wrong.

I attribute lack of money management skills, poor financial knowledge, and young irresponsibility to my failure. Because of those factors, I did not take full advantage of the powerful opportunities I was given by God. I was the epitome of young and foolish, living my twenties as if I had all the time and money in the world. My decisions were immature, and I would frequently blow money on parties, shoes, jewelry, cars, trips, while also helping family and friends. At the end of the day, I wasted my money, never setting aside funds for emergencies, investing in insurance or my future. Those decisions came back to haunt me when my store was burglarized one day. The thieves took everything, emptying my store completely. The lack of insurance made the situation even worse and I was forced to sell my business for pennies on the dollar literally next to nothing. That ended one of the most important chapters of my life and left me devastated.

I would love to share a life changing story with you. My clothing store was held in a rented storefront. When it came time to hand over the keys to the building's owner, my heart was filled with regret and sorrow. That day changed my life FOREVER. The owner of the building was a successful real estate investor who showed sympathy at my plight. As I passed over the keys, I could not stop the tears from welling up in my eyes. Seeing this, he asked if I was doing alright. I told him I honestly felt like a huge failure. Surprisingly, he said in so many words, "young man, you did not fail. Every time I came to this store it felt like Grand Central Station. Business was booming and beyond successful. On top of that you made a lot of money and took a risk by opening a business in one of the most dangerous parts of the city and succeeded. *If I may, the main problem I saw was that you live in a 'CASH IS KING' world and Cash is King of a very small kingdom. CREDIT IS THE RULER OF THE UNIVERSE.* Would you rather rule a small kingdom or rule a universe?" That conversation changed my life's trajectory, my mindset, and my life itself FOREVER!!!!!

At first, I did not understand what he meant but his words sparked the desire to learn everything I possibly could about **CREDIT.** If I was a mob boss, Credit had just had a hit put on him. ***What was it? Where did it come from? How did it work? Why does it work that way? How do I use it?*** I needed to know every detail about credit. I spent hours every day researching credit. I read books, Googled articles, watched videos, and talked to those around me for their insights as well. "Babe did you know credit could...?" and "Honey, guess what I learned about credit..." became frequent conversation starters with my wife. I was like a man obsessed, and she definitely called me out on it as well. She may have gone crazy if I talked about credit any more than I did. But that is the point. I urge you to also become obsessed with it, or at the very least learn as much as you possibly can. ***Understanding credit changed my life and I know it can do the same for you***.

Now, let us fast forward to the future just a bit. At this point in time, you have whipped your personal credit into shape, your business credit is looking great, you have opened the business of your choice, and it is time to move forward. Now, it is time to start **BUILDING YOUR CASTLE.** In my personal, opinion of all the ways you can use a good credit file, none is as important as using it to **OWN PROPERTY.** In my experience, owning property is where the real money is made. To begin, I advise owning the property that your business is based out of and you can use your credit to do that. It is a fantastic investment. Now, that does not mean going out and buying a huge commercial space, but rather consider purchasing a mixed-use property. A property that has a storefront on the first floor and apartments above it is a great investment. Why? You now have a rent-free space to conduct business and you can rent out the above apartments to generate even more income. That income can then be used to cover the mortgage on the property. Doing this also allows overhead operating costs to be cut. Think about it, now there are multiple sources of income all from one investment. Renting the apartments can cover the mortgage while your business is still generating, well, business. If a shop of some sort is what you desire, this is a great route for you to consider. The final, takeaway own the building your business is in and well owning property.

Connecting your business to a real estate transaction is a crucial step in building **GENERATIONAL WEALTH**. That building can now be passed down to your kids, leaving them assets rather than liabilities in the future. On top of that, owning real estate is a major accomplishment. Combining two investments that will secure the other is a great move, keep in mind if the apartments are going unoccupied for some time, the business can help cover the mortgage; and while the apartments are occupied, the incoming rent will keep operational costs of the business minimized.

Making such an investment can change the direction of your life forever. You are now also beginning to change the lives of your future family and loved ones as well. While businesses succeed and fail, owning properties is a different ball game altogether. To be frank, it is the game that has produced countless millionaires throughout this country and the world. Making these decisions and building a real estate portfolio can lead to wealth that lasts a lifetime.

If anyone can attribute a motto to me, it would be *USE REAL ESTATE TO FUND YOUR DREAMS."* I personally live by those words and it is my desire to see those words work for you as well. *Grow your real estate portfolio, focus on building residual income, and own as much property as you can; let real estate pay for your lifestyle.*

One last thing I want you to know is that making this happen does not have to be difficult. To begin, find a mortgage broker and obtain a pre-approval. The job of the broker is to tell you how much financing you qualify for in order to purchase property. They will assist you in gathering the necessary documents and explain the process of obtaining the financing you need. In the resources section of this book, you will find the contact information to a preferred mortgage broker. After getting pre-approved, you will want to find a real estate broker to assist you in finding the ideal property for you. Therefore, in the resources section of this book, you will find the contact information for a preferred real estate broker as well. Understand that the mortgage broker helps you secure a loan and a real estate broker will help you find the perfect property. Keep in mind that guidelines vary from state to state in regards to financing and purchasing, but either way, credit will play an integral role no matter your location.

OWN THE BUILDING.

OWN YOUR BUSINESS.

BUILD YOUR CASTLE!

The idea is to use your credit to create opportunities for yourself rather than bad debt. The building you purchase will be considered a debt but know that it is what I call "good debt". What is good debt? Any type of investment that will generate income such as a rental property, purchasing equipment and supplies for a business, etc. What is bad debt? Shopping sprees and unnecessary vacations funded by your credit cards. Make sure to always use your credit effectively and wisely.

CHAPTER 7
RULE THE UNIVERSE

RULER OF THE UNIVERSE

As the newly crowned King or Queen of the castle, do not allow complacency to settle in as there will always be more work to be done. **Cash is King, but Credit is the Ruler of the Universe.** With that, being said...

PROTECT YOUR CREDIT!!!!

If your credit was utilized to make investments, be sure that those investments will pay back the debt you accumulated on your credit.

Moving forward, keeping your credit strong and intact is vital to your business. You can protect your credit by at the very least making the minimum required payments on all credit cards. Do not neglect to pay any installment loans as well. Always be certain that these payments are being made **ON TIME**.

Beyond protecting your credit, making your payments consistently and on time will help you build a strong relationship with the banks and lenders you are borrowing from. Quoting the late and great Nipsey Hustle once more, **"I got a team at my bank. I don't even need an ID at my bank."** What does that mean? Simple, building and having a relationship with your lenders or bankers will give you the advantages you need to grow your business. Finding a banker who is knowledgeable and has your best interest at heart is an invaluable tool. Also keep in mind that you should work with a bank that has lending programs that you can take advantage of. Building a rapport with your banker will expose you to those programs and help propel your business far into the future. Remember, good credit can, and most likely will, be your best investor, allowing you to capitalize on each, and every opportunity that comes your way.

Being the King or Queen of your kingdom is a great accomplishment and if you are happy and satisfied with that, then you have already won. Why stop there? Especially since being the **Ruler of Your Universe** is where your ultimate, goal should lie. Now, will becoming the ruler of your own universe be an easy task? Not by a long shot. It will take hard work, dedication, and plenty of sacrifices. There will be sleepless nights, setbacks, and obstacles to overcome, and challenges that must be faced. It is how you face those challenges that will determine what type of ruler you are going to be. It is also those challenges that will give you the knowledge and experience you will need to be the **Best Version of Yourself.** You might fall and you might fail but recall that with failure comes lessons. Some of the biggest blessings will follow those hard and difficult lessons.

You must continue your journey and continue to level up, as your future quite literally depends on it. Grow and keep growing, push and keep pushing. Do not be afraid to get smarter, better, and stronger because when you know better, you are able to do better. Keep your vision in mind and always remember **WHY** you are doing what you are doing. **Knowing Your WHYS** and your reasons means you will be able to reflect on those values to keep you going when times get tough. You have a dream to become the Ruler of Your Universe, not simply the King or Queen of your Kingdom.

Becoming the ruler of your universe entails being the ruler of yourself and knowing who you are, who you want to be, and why. Learn your strengths and weaknesses and improve upon them both. Study yourself, master yourself, and eventually you will rule yourself. You can create the life that you always wanted and dreamed of. You can accomplish your goals by being serious about them. *Use the Power of Credit to help you*. If you worked to build it up, make it work for you to help you build up your future. You have the knowledge and you have the tools you need to do it. So, do it. *Just Make It Happen! BE THE RULER OF YOUR UNIVERSE!*

SPREAD THE WEALTH

SPREAD THE WEALTH

Now that you have reached your goals, made your dreams come true, and created the life you want for you and your loved ones, your job is done. Right? Not by a longshot. At this point, you still have work to do and it is time to **SPREAD THE WEALTH**. No, this is not me telling you to give away your money. I simply mean that it is now time to give back. Spread your knowledge, spread your resources, and spread your network; share your knowledge and teach others who wish to learn, **ESPECIALLY THE YOUTH.** Show them the steps you took, what methods worked for you, and the pitfalls that you encountered so that they may avoid them. As we all know by now, knowledge is power, and sharing knowledge means sharing that power. Helping others will not only benefit them, but is also a phenomenal way to network, create connections, and build bridges that you may have to cross later in life.

I once watched a movie entitled "Lucy" starring Morgan Freeman and Scarlett Johannsson. If you are not familiar with the film then here come some spoilers. The movie is essentially about a woman who was exposed to some chemicals/drugs that granted her the ability to use one hundred percent of her brain power. The more brain power she utilized, the stronger she became, both mentally and physically. I introduce this film to you because it was a movie that honestly resonated with me. The main character, Lucy, asked Morgan Freeman's character, **"What am I supposed to do with all of this knowledge?"** She referred to the knowledge granted to her through being able to use so much of her brain power at once. Morgan Freeman's character responded, *"Well, You Pass It On."* That simple answer honestly changed the direction and focus of my life. Knowledge is meant to be passed on from one to another, from *Generation to Generation.* That is the task I have chosen for myself and the task I am asking you to take up as well.

It seems to me that many people are taught to keep their connections and resources a secret, a treasure trove for only themselves. Do not be that way. Helping others can grant a sense of accomplishment beyond belief. Putting someone else in a position to win is just as important as winning for yourself. Playing basketball is a favorite recreation of mine and one of my favorite things to do when playing is to Assist. In basketball, an assist occurs when you pass the ball to your teammate and they score. I get just as much satisfaction out of the pass than I do from simply scoring myself. Make sure you surround yourself with people who think the same way. Do not surround yourself with ball-hogs; build a team that will throw you an assist, give you an alley oop. One more sports analogy, just to drive this point home, is considering the position of the quarterback in football. The quarterback's primary goal is to throw the ball or hand it off to another player to score a touchdown. I love this position for the exact same reason: I am throwing the ball or handing it off for a teammate to score and receive credit. The same goes for real-life knowledge and resources.

There is Power in Numbers. Unity is vital and together we are strong. Those are my philosophies because there is nothing more powerful than a group of people working together towards a Common Goal. I never go into any kind of relationship or partnership looking for what I can get out of it; rather, go in with the mindset of *"How can I help as well."* That mindset is what leads to true growth in business and personal relationships.

Be a Mentor. Being the person that others look to for guidance, knowledge, and advice is a wonderful thing. *Find a Mentor*. Having someone you can talk to is a great way to limit mistakes and keep you on the right track. The way to break generational curses is to pass on the knowledge so that the same mistakes are not repeated by future generations. The way to create generational wealth is to acquire assets that can be passed on to others. Your kids should not have to start at the same place you started. Your grandkids should love you for *CREATING FAMILY WEALTH,*

GENERATIONAL WEALTH.

Becoming the ruler of your universe goes much deeper than simply ruling your universe and creating your businesses. It is about creating wealth for your family that will follow them well into the future. Make it your life mission to obtain as much knowledge and acquire as many *Cash Flowing Assets* to pass down to your family. Earlier in this chapter, I said I did not want you to go around giving your money away. At the end of the day, however, that is exactly what I am telling you to do. You want to be able to leave your family a fortune that will exist long after you have left this world.

SPREAD THE WEALTH!

CHAPTER 9
IN A NUTSHELL

IN A NUTSHELL

The life of an entrepreneur can drive you crazy, becoming an obsession that can very, likely take you to the brink of insanity. In fact, I was at one of the lowest, darkest points in my life when I discovered the **Importance of Credit.** To be honest, I was homeless, but blessed enough to be living rent free in my friend Mr. Carters apartment. To complicate matters, my girlfriend – who is now my wife – was pregnant and I was starting over after being forced to sell my store for pennies on the dollar. To say that I was depressed and confused is an understatement. I was also worried and terrified that I would never financially recover. I was completely lost. Starting over is horrifying especially from scratch with nothing.

I clearly remember the day that my life changed forever. I had fifteen dollars to my name: five dollars went towards gas for my car. After that, I went to a friend's liquor store and bought a cheap bottle of vodka and a bag of chips for $5.50. This friend was someone I owed quite a lot of money to, ten thousand dollars, in fact, from a failed business venture. When I walked in, the first thing he asked was when could he expect his money back. Being in the dark mindset I was in my response was less than pleasant. I told him that I did not have the money and that he could expect it when I had it. Give or take a few more nasty words and a darker tone, and you get the gist of my response. Even though I was depressed it was during this time I was **Studying**

Credit and Real Estate, which go hand and hand. So, I told him that if he wanted me to give him his ten thousand back to give me another ten-thousand and I would pay him back his twenty thousand plus interest. In an equally nasty and explicit manner, he laughed at me and told me ***NO.***

So now I have $4.50 to my name and a bad taste in my mouth from the confrontation. On the way home, I buy my girlfriend and son a double cheeseburger and small fries each. The total was $4.48; I did not have enough to buy myself anything to eat. The bag of chips and the vodka were all I had to eat that day, but I could not regret the alcohol: it was the only way to ease my mental anguish at the time. After, I went home and took a shower, and it was while I was in the shower that I got down on my knees and prayed. I cried out to God in my mind, ***HELP ME!*** I know it is said that God works on his own time but in my prayer, I begged him to ***HELP ME NOW!!!*** I needed him at that moment, not later or in some mysterious, distant future. I had no money, no food, and a hint of gas in my car. My life felt over because I could not provide for myself or my family. As I got out of the shower and wiped away my tears, before I could finish drying off, my phone rang. It was my friend, the one who owned the liquor store and whom I had just exchanged a few harsh words with. I instantly became frustrated at seeing his name on my caller ID, assuming he was calling to harass me about the money again. Something told me to pick up the phone even though I had no intention of doing so. When I said hello, he said "What's Up?" as if I had not just exchanged unpleasantries with him. He then asked me why I wanted the ten-thousand dollars, and I immediately urged him to forget all about it. Instead, he continued to ask me why I wanted the money. After asking him to forget that I even asked a few times he told me to come pick the money up from his store the next day. I did not understand what was happening, but it was **God Answering My Prayers.** I went on to buy my first house for **$8.500.00** and the rest, as they say, is history.

The journey of a dreamer is not easy, and it is not for everyone. I made the decision to pursue it and I stick with that decision. Good or bad, right, or wrong, through success or failure, I wake up every day and chase my dreams. Regardless of the obstacles placed in front of me, I refuse to give up because *failure is simply not an option*. It cannot be. *Failure can only occur when you quit*, and I cannot do that. I urge you to never quit either. Remember, if you quit, it is failure; if you keep going and learn, it is a lesson. The lifestyle can drive you crazy and is a non-stop, roller coaster ride with insane twists and turns and crazy ups and downs. That is okay, though. *Keep going.*

To wrap and recap:

Do not give up on your goals or dreams, keep chasing them. It is never too late to go after what you want or to be who you want to be. Someone once told me, you can either be forty, fifty, or sixty years old and doing what you want to do, or you can be forty, fifty, or sixty years old anyway and be full of regrets. Either way, if you can see it, you can achieve it.

Find a Balance in your life when it comes to setting goals and pursuing them. Create some stability because it will make your journey easier. Take care of yourself mentally and physically as well and rely on your family and friends throughout your journey. Afterall, what good is living the dream if you are alone or burn yourself out trying to reach THE DREAM.

Keep in mind that only you can Guarantee Your Success. Make strides towards getting your Personal Credit in order. Use the Power of Credit App to assist you. Get your free Analysis and Consultation, find the areas you need to work on and GET TO WORK. Use the Dispute letters in the resource section in the back of this book. When you put in the work, you will reap the rewards.

Do not wait for an opportunity to come knocking on the door and do not keep knocking on the door waiting for someone else to answer it. Make your own door and your own keys so you can Unlock the Doors. Be prepared to take advantage of any opportunity that comes your way. Take control of your life and your destiny and be who you were made to be.

Make sure that you **Invest in Yourself** by leveraging your credit to create opportunities. After strengthening your personal credit, obtain business credit and let both, of them put you in the game. If you are in the game, you have a chance to win, but you do not get a win unless you first play the game. Bet on Yourself; you know what you want to do and what you have, to do. Even if others do not share your vision, that is alright. Your success depends on you because when all is said and done, it is Your Dream.

Be the King or Queen of your castle – be your Own Boss. That means owning the business, owning the building, owning the rights or the patent, or whatever it is you are pursuing. Ownership is the ONLY WAY. You are in control of whether you succeed or fail, and failure cannot be an option.

Always focus on continual growth. Create a goal, accomplish it, and the create another. Rule Your Universe by knowing yourself. Study your strengths and weaknesses, master them, and work towards becoming the best version of yourself that you can possibly be. You have the power of the universe with you and within you.

Finally, it is our responsibility to help each other. Help the next person master themselves. Teach the next generation what you have learned. Share your experiences, share your resources, share your network, and share your knowledge. Spread the Wealth. Help others to reach their goals like you have reached yours; assist them in reaching their full potential as you continually strive to reach yours. **Remember, it is a Blessing to be a Blessing.**

IN A NUTSHELL!

OUTRO

That is the sole purpose of this book, to be a blessing.

I hope and pray that this information can help you in any way. That this book finds you in good health, strong mind, and in good spirit. I pray that all your goals are met and that all your dreams come true. May God bless you with what your heart desires and grants you Peace, Love, and Prosperity.

God Bless you and the rest of the world.

Best and warmest regards,

Tony Santos

POWER OF CREDIT LLC

SAMPLE LETTER

Today's Date

Your Full Name (Make sure it matches the name on your credit report)

City, State, Zip

SSN: 000-00-0000 | DOB: 0/0/0000

Credit Bureau Address

This letter is to inform you that I recently received a copy of my credit report that your company publishes and after reviewing it I found a number of items on the report that are inaccurate. The accounts in question are listed below. Please send me copies of the documents that you have in your files as of this date that you used to verify the accuracy of the accounts listed below.

Under the Fair Credit Reporting Act, 15 U.S.C. § 1681g I have the right to demand that you disclose to me all of the documents that you have recorded and retained in your file at the time of this request concerning the accounts that you are reporting in my credit report. Please don't respond to my request by saying that these accounts have been verified. Send me copies of the documents that you have in your files that were used to verify them. If you do not have any documentation in your files to verify the accuracy of these disputed accounts, then please delete them immediately as required under Section611(a)(5)(A)(i). By publishing these inaccurate and unverified items on my credit report and distributing to 3rd parties you are damaging my reputation and credit worthiness.

Under the FCRA 15 U.S.C. § 1681i, all unverified accounts must be promptly deleted. Therefore, if you are unable to provide me with a copy of the verifiable proof that you have on file for each of the accounts listed below within 30 days of receipt of this letter then you must remove these accounts from my credit reports.

Please provide me with a copy of an updated and corrected credit report showing these items removed, I demand the following accounts be properly verified or removed immediately.

Name of Account: Verification:	Account Number:	Provide Physical Proof of
Company Name	XXXXXX XXXXXX	Unverified Account

* NOTE: Please also remove all non-account holding inquiries over 30 days old.

Thank You, Sign your name here (Your Name Here) attach: Copy of your Social Security Card and Driver's License Send: USPS Certified Mail.

POWER OF CREDIT LLC.
BUSINESS PUNCHLIST

1. NAME & ADDRESS & START DATE OF THE BUSINESS

2. REGISTER BUSINESS WITH SECRETARY OF STATE

3. OBTAIN EIN/TAX ID FROM IRS

4. PHONE LINE FOR BUSINESS USE ONLY

5. REGISTERED PHONE NUMBER WITH 411

6. PROFESSIONAL BUSINESS EMAIL

7. WEBSITE

8. BUSINESS BANK ACCOUNT

9. MERCHANT ACCOUNT

NOTE: THE FOLLOWING ARE HIGHLY RECOMMENDED:

PROFESSIONAL VOICEMAIL, LOGO, FAX NUMBER, 800 NUMBER, PROFESSIONAL LICENSES, BUSINESS PERMITS.

POWER OF CREDIT

BUSINESS CREDIT SERVICE SUMMARY

1. Start/Structure Corporate Entity

2. Register Corporation with Business Credit Reporting Agencies

3. Strategically apply for Corporate Credit (Round 1)

4. Monitor Corporate Credit Reports (3 months)

5. Strategically apply for Corporate Credit (Round 2)

6. Monitor Corporate Credit Reports (3 months)

7. Establish Perfect Corporate Credit Score (Paydex Score)

8. Strategically apply for Corporate Credit (Round 3)

9. Strategically apply for Business Loans (Round 3)

Note: The Business Credit Program is A 3 to 12month program that involves different levels of financing and funding. If the business goes through the full 12month process, the business will have the ability to qualify for financing that does not require a Personal Guarantor. The business will be able to stand on its own CREDIT POWER.

POWER OF CREDIT SERVICES

- CREDIT ANALYSIS
- CREDIT CONSULTATION
- CREDIT RESTORATION
- CREDIT ENHANCEMENT
- CREDIT FUNDING
- CREDIT SEMINARS
- ONE ON ONE COACHING
- BUSINESS START UP
- BUSINESS CREDIT BUILDING
- BUSINESS CREDIT FUNDING
- BUSINESS PLAN DEVELOPMENT
- BUSINESS COACHING
- FINANCIAL LITERACY EDUCATION
- WEALTH DEVELOPMENT PROGRAMS
- REAL ESTAE INVESTMENT COACHING

POWER OF CREDIT

TOP CREDIT TIPS

Credit Tips You Should Know

- Pay more than the minimum payment on Credit Cards.
- Make all your monthly payments on time.
- Never go over 30% on your Credit Card Balances.
- Pay all Credit Cards to below 30% before the reporting date.
- Keep older accounts in good standing OPEN.
- Check your credit report at least once a month.
- Don't Co-sign for anybody (Sorry Mom).
- Don't use credit for everyday life expenses.
- Use credit to create opportunity, Not debt.
- Learn as much as you can about credit.
- Put some sort of Identity Theft Protection on you file.
- Teach the youth what you KNOW about CREDIT.
- Credit is one of your Biggest Assets PROTECT IT.

CREDIT BUREAUS CONTACT INFORMATION

Trans Union Consumer Relations,

P.O. Box 2000,

Chester, PA 19016.

Dispute Items and Status Checks 800-916-8800

www.transunion.com

Experian National Consumer Assistance Center,

P.O. Box 4500 Allen, TX 75013

Dispute Credit Report Items 800-509-8495

www.experian.com

Equifax Credit Information Services, LLC

P.O. Box 740256 Atlanta, GA 30348

Dispute Credit Report Items 866-349-5191

www.equifax.com

*For your one free copy of your report from all 3 bureaus once a year. www.annualcreditreport.com

POWER OF CREDIT

SUMMARY OF RIGHTS (FCRA)

1. You must be told if information in your file has been used against you.

2. You have the Right to know what is in your file.

3. You have the right to ask for a credit score.

4. You have the right to dispute incomplete of inaccurate information.

5. Consumer reporting agencies must correct or delete inaccurate,

incomplete or unverified information,

6. Consumer agencies may not report outdated negative information.

7. Access to your file is limited.

8. You must give your consent for reports to be provided to your employers.

9. You may limit offers of credit and insurance you get based on the

information in your credit report.

10. You may seek damages from violators.

11. Identity theft victims and active duty personnel have additional rights

States may enforce the FCRA, and many states have their own consumer reporting laws. In some cases, you may have more rights under state law. For more information, contact your state or local consumer protection agency or your state Attorney General.

Real Estate Resources

Company: HomeSmart Connect

Real Estate Broker: Tammy Knighten

Phone Number: 1-312-912-1361

Email Address: tammyyouragent@gmail.com

Company: Fairway Mortgage

Mortgage Broker: Steve Butler

Phone Number:1-708-308-2947

Email: steve.mtg11@gmail.com

Company: Guaranteed Rate

Mortgage Broker: Guy Petropoulos

Phone Number: 1-312-287-9866

Email: guy.petropoulos@rate.com

Company: Migdal Law Group

Attorney: Perry Perelman

Phone Number:1-847-630-1477

Email: perry@migdallawgroup.com

POWER OF CREDIT
CONTACT INFORMATION

Tony Santos

Power of Credit LLC

6955 W North Ave. Unit 202

Oak Park IL. 60302

Office line - 888-859-1465

Direct Line - 773-567-2738

Email: tony@powerofcredit.com

NOTES

NOTES